Mothering Your Special Child

A Book for Mothers or Carers of Children Diagnosed with Asperger Syndrome

JOSIE SANTOMAURO

Illustrated by Carla Marino

Jessica Kingsley Publishers
London and Philadelphia

First published in 2009
by Jessica Kingsley Publishers
116 Pentonville Road
London N1 9JB, UK
and
400 Market Street, Suite 400
Philadelphia, PA 19106, USA

www.jkp.com

Hampshire County Library	
C014678215	
Askews	Jul-2010
618.92858832	£9.99
	9781843106579

Library of Congress Cataloging in Publication Data
Santomauro, J. (Josie)
    Mothering your special child : a book for mothers or carers of children diagnosed with
asperger syndrome / Josie Santomauro ; iIllustrated by Carla Marino.
        p. cm.
    ISBN 978-1-84310-657-9 (pb : alk. paper) 1. Asperger's syndrome--Popular works.
2. Asperger's syndrome--Patients--Family relationships. 3. Parents of autistic children. 4.
Caregivers. 5. Mothers. I. Marino, Carla. II. Title.
    RJ506.A9S364 2009
    618.92'858832--dc22
                                                    2008041284

British Library Cataloguing in Publication Data
A CIP catalogue record for this book is available from the British Library

ISBN 978 1 84310 657 9

Printed and bound in Great Britain by
Athenaeum Press, Gateshead, Tyne and Wear

MOTHERING YOUR SPECIAL CHILD

To all mothers of persons with
Asperger Syndrome

I wish to thank all the wonderful
contributors who have given
permission to reprint their gifts of
poetry, reflections, writings and
private thoughts here in this
book.

Contributors hold the original
copyrights to their work.

Contents

Introduction

I congratulate you on reaching this point, to move on from the initial diagnosis of your child having Asperger Syndrome.

Your child may have been given the diagnosis of Asperger Syndrome by a pediatrician, psychologist, speech therapist, teacher or friend. I hope that you were dealt the news in a compassionate and positive way.

Diagnosis is the first hurdle and there will be many more hurdles in your child's life. The end result is the satisfaction that you were there for your child. Friends, doctors, teachers will come and go, but you will be the stability in his/her life, and you will have made a difference. Your role is not only to help your child understand, accept and love the world, but to help people around your child to understand, accept and love 'his/her' world.

Although Asperger Syndrome may appear to consume your life sometimes (well, most of the time) try not to dwell on the negatives, love the positives and embrace your child's successes.

When my son was first diagnosed, little was known about Asperger Syndrome, particularly for parents. Whilst preparing this book I have found that I was constantly revisiting my grief, and I have found the process to be a wonderful vehicle for therapy.

The aim of this book is to introduce Asperger Syndrome to you in a positive light, and to guide you, the mother, through some issues that you may face on the Asperger Syndrome journey with your child.

My son, Damian, was diagnosed 13 years ago, at the age of five, therefore I am able to share my first-hand experiences. We can learn from those who have already started this journey as I have learned from others also. I encourage you to research and learn as much about Asperger Syndrome as you can, to equip yourself with the tools to support your child.

Best wishes and good luck!

What is Asperger Syndrome?

There are various ways of defining Asperger Syndrome. I can only offer you basic information on the diagnostic area, but a wealth of information based on my experiences. I encourage you to seek further information from specialists in this area, support groups, other parents, the internet and other resources. Knowledge is power – I can't state this enough. The more you learn, the more adept you will become in handling your child's journey.

Throughout this book you will find Asperger Syndrome referred to as AS, and sometimes as an ASD. ASD is an abbreviation for autistic spectrum disorder. Asperger Syndrome falls within the autistic spectrum.

On first meeting someone we make a number of judgements. We can tell their age and a lot about their character from their appearance, and we can tell from facial expressions and tone of voice what mood they are in. This enables us to react to them in an appropriate way.

People with AS don't find it so easy to recognize this information, and because they find eye contact difficult it is hard for them to interact easily with other people.

However, once they are diagnosed with AS, these difficulties can be understood and dealt with, and the benefits of AS can be appreciated.

What's wrong with my child?

Your child needs extra assistance in these four areas:

1. Social skills

2. Communication

3. Behaviour

4. Sensory stimulation.

Social skills

Two-way social interaction may be impaired due to the inability of your child to understand the rules of social behaviour. There may be little or no eye contact used when listening or speaking. A lack of empathy may be shown to others and to others' interests/activities, unless they are of specific interest to your child.

Communication

Your child may speak at the appropriate age, but sometimes speech can be delayed. Speech may be pedantic and/or repetitive. Usually there are comprehension difficulties with verbal instructions, etc. He/she tends to be a very visual thinker and learner.

Behaviour

Your child may become obsessive about particular possessions or objects. Preferring life to be predictable they don't cope well with change in situations, structure or routine. They may not cope well with verbal instructions, therefore to avoid negative feedback they may become defiant in their behaviour.

Sensory stimulation

Your child may have difficulty focusing attention due to hyper- or hypo-sensory input in the environment (e.g. they may need headphones in noisy places). They may need sensory experiences during the day (e.g. stress balls or other fidget items).

Common features of Asperger Syndrome

A nger and frustration

S tress and anxiety

P roblems with speech and language

E asily distracted

R eality/Fiction confusion

G ross motor skills

E ccentric or odd behaviours

R igid and resistant to change

S ocial skills deficit

Y our child may be intelligent

N o or little eye contact

D oesn't like loud noises and crowds

R ote memory strong

O bsessional interests

M aking friends may be difficult

E mpathy – lack of

Let's take a closer look at Asperger Syndrome

Anger and frustration

- Your child may have temper tantrums or anger outbursts.

- They might find it hard to ask for help when feeling confused or frustrated.

Stress and anxiety

- They don't cope well with being teased or bullied.
- They are sometimes anxious over changes.
- They are often very stressed at school.
- They don't cope well with criticism or failure.

Problems with speech and language

- They may not realize that their voice is too loud.
- They may have a monotone voice or an unusual accent.
- They may require some speech therapy.
- They may have difficulty explaining what they want to say.

Easily distracted

- Maybe their room and school desk is untidy.

- They may have short-term memory problems.

- It can be hard for them to pay attention or focus.

Reality/Fiction confusion

- Sometimes they don't understand jokes or stories.

- They may believe that their dreams are real.

- They take things literally, such as 'pull your socks up', and don't understand sarcasm.

Gross motor skills

- They may appear clumsy or have an odd gait.
- They may have poor co-ordination and find some sports (especially ball games) challenging.

Eccentric or odd behaviours

- They may have eccentric/odd behaviours.
- They may have eccentric/odd collections/hobbies.

Rigid and resistant to change

- They prefer routine and structure.
- They work best when forewarned about events.
- They may not work well with transitions.

Social skills deficit

- They may find it hard to understand people's body language.
- They need help to ignore teasing and bullying.

- They may be unaware of social rules and can sometimes appear rude.

Your child may be intelligent

- They can be very intelligent – especially at maths, science and computers.

- They are nicknamed 'little professor' by some professionals.

No or little eye contact

- They don't like looking into people's eyes when they talk to them and may look at the ground instead of someone's face.

- They may find the ground more interesting than your face but they are still listening to what you are saying.

Doesn't like loud noises and crowds

- They are sensitive to sensory stimuli.

- Noisy or crowded places, like shopping centres or parties, can overload their sensory system.

Rote memory strong

- Excellent long-term memory.

- Walking encyclopedia for specific facts.

Obsessional interests

- An obsession with a particular hobby/subject can dominate conversations, play and daily life.

- Repetitive movements, e.g. flapping their hands, touching their face or blinking.

Making friends may be difficult

- They might not have many friends and find it hard to make new friends.

- They may not have a desire to have friends, they may prefer to be on their own.

- They may prefer to play with older or younger people.

Empathy – lack of

- Sometimes they can't understand how other people are feeling.

- They may find it difficult to understand facial expressions.

Here's another acrostic to show some other characteristics of Asperger Syndrome:

A rtistic

S mart

P unctual

E ngaging

R epetitive movements

G ood natured

E xtraordinary

R ules

S ignificant

Y why? Asks lots of questions

N atural

D etermined

R esourceful

O ver sensitive

M aths wiz

E motional

Good Grief

When a mother is told their child has a disability they need to go through the classic stages of grief. If we put the process on hold we may find that a breakdown may eventually hit years later.

Grief is the natural healing process of a loss. You as a mother will grieve the news of your child's diagnosis. I have found whilst putting this book together that I have revisited the early years and unearthed issues of grief that I obviously put aside years ago.

It's healthy to grieve. It's a health hazard to bury your emotions.

Grief comes with a sense of loss, of a loved one, a job, pet, home or physical action. Even aging can cause grief. So the grief you experience at the loss of the 'normality' of your child can have the same impact as those other losses. A diagnosis of a disability, disease or life-threatening illness can have a devastating effect on not only you, but also the whole family.

The diagnosis of your child with Asperger Syndrome can have the same impact on you as news of a death.

The grieving process begins, and it is important that you are allowed to grieve in your own way. Take the necessary time to grieve, without pressure to 'pick yourself up'. It is very important that support is in place to assist your grieving process along.

These are some feelings/behaviours you may be experiencing:

- denial
- shock
- anger
- guilt
- regret
- depression
- loneliness.

There are many changes about to happen in your life. You will gradually learn to understand and accommodate these changes and move on to a different path.

The stages of grief are denial, anger, sadness and then, finally, acceptance.

Denial: The initial shock. It's difficult to believe what you've just been told. 'This can't be happening to me.'

Anger: The most difficult stage. 'It's not fair, why me?' This stage introduces feelings of guilt: 'What have I done to deserve this?' Self-blame may become a problem, or you may blame doctors, schools, etc. Your anger may also be directed at the child.

Sadness: The essential ingredient of the grieving process. Cry, cry and more crying, it's good for you, don't hold back, and don't swallow it.

Acceptance: Resuming life. Getting back to the way things were prior to diagnosis but on a different level. This is the sign that the grieving process is nearing the end.

It may take you more than six months to grieve or it may take some years, but the process is essential. Blocking it or not allowing yourself to grieve will only create problems, e.g. breakdown/depression occurring many years later. Your friends and family may try to make you feel better by saying things like: 'It's not the end of the world'/'Life goes on'/'Be strong'. These aren't exactly the things you want to hear at the time, but they mean well. You really just want them to understand your pain. You don't want them to solve your problem. Find a friend or support group who will help you with this and who will listen to you.

How did my child get Asperger Syndrome?

We don't really know the exact answer to this question.

It may be genetic, it may be due to the mother contracting a virus whilst pregnant, or it may be that the child contracts a virus in their first year.

With our son, it could be any or all three!

1. We think there may be some family members with mild traits.

2. At 22 weeks pregnant, I contracted a virus and was hospitalized due to dehydration.

3. At 11 months, Damian contracted the measles virus (one month before he was due for the immunization!). He was a very sick little boy, and it took him about two months to recover. When he did get better, he reverted to crawling.

Asperger Syndrome is not caught like a cold, that glass of wine does not cause it during your pregnancy, and it's not because your child fell and hit their head. There have been many studies done and research is ongoing. Some say it's possibly due to immunizations, some say there's a possible dietary factor. Until the day the discovery of the cause is officially announced, I believe we should just move on and deal with the symptoms.

What we do know is that there is at least one in every 150 people who has Asperger Syndrome and, most importantly, through communication with adults with Asperger Syndrome, we do know how to make their lives easier.

We now have to teach the world how to accept them and their ways.

Been There, Done That

Learning from those who have been there before, those who have paved the way (whether they be other mothers or adults with ASD), can be powerful knowledge as well as reassuring to those just beginning to find their feet.

I have found that the words from adults with ASD are precious, and by listening to them we can be guided with our decision-making when confronted by situations with our own children.

Our personal experience

Six years ago, my son was diagnosed at age nine with mild Asperger Syndrome. He had experienced extreme school anxiety and depression as well as some phobias. He has come a long way in working his way through these obstacles. I would like to share some of my observations from our journey.

I have noticed the frustration and guilt that parents often go through in trying to sift through all the different choices that come before them. We agonized over whether to send our child to school or to home school, whether to give him a particular medication, vaccination, food supplementation, special diet, method of discipline/therapy to use; the list goes on. Often guilt over a past choice may linger if we see no improvement, or fear may arise if we are faced with new choices that we are unfamiliar with.

From my own personal experiences and observations over the years, I have come to realize that at each step, each individual family must make the choice that seems the best at that time.

As important as each choice may seem, there is an even more crucial factor than the choice itself – love. It sometimes can seem overwhelming when we list the pros and cons and feel that if we make the 'wrong' choice, our child loses time, or worse, remains lost forever. The most significant factor that I have ever witnessed in the positive growth and development of any child is the underlying support and encouragement of a loving family.

Whatever the choice at whatever particular stage, we should undertake it with gentleness and love. That's the crucial ingredient. Whether we feel home schooling or a public school is best for our child at the moment is an individual decision. But whichever one we decide is best, it will be invalidated, or worse, a negative experience for all, if it is carried through grudgingly. The loving commitment and support that we transmit to our child is the key to opening the door.

In our own journey with our son we have come upon various 'difficult' choices concerning schooling, medication, counselling, therapies, etc. Sometimes we agreed with schools or psychiatrists, sometimes not. There were often 'advantages' of a path we didn't choose to take – yet we felt at that time that a different path was more comfortable, convenient or reasonable for our family situation as a whole...so many factors. We know that we need to be flexible enough to change a direction when we feel it is no longer useful. We also try to be open to ideas that we might not have considered before. We know not to get stuck in guilt or regret, but to learn from any mistakes and move on. Above all, we embrace the challenge of loving our son into becoming all that he can be.

Laura Gilbert (USA) Mother of
a teenager with Asperger Syndrome

Asperger never leaves

Asperger Syndrome if you have it never leaves, in actual fact it never gets better! There is no cure, but as we get older we learn new ways around corners.

Circumstances alter and we may be given advice in coping strategies and that is what it is, just coping. In the end, we devise methods of getting around those corners on our own. Sometimes we do it well, sometimes not, but anybody who lives in close contact knows that we have not really changed, but that we still have those problems.

It is only those people who are not close to us that can be fooled. The key words here being 'close to us', as we tend not to develop closeness with many people.

Rest assured that the day will never dawn when you will awaken to find ASD on any level gone.

Yes, your child will probably need help in mainstream school, and as he gets older will probably need more help, not less.

Nanna Shirl (Gin Gin, Australia)
'An old dyed in the wool – age early seventies' with
Asperger Syndrome

When I was younger I always knew that I was different

As a young person recently diagnosed with Asperger Syndrome, I find it increasingly difficult for non-autistic people to understand what Asperger Syndrome is. It would be like someone I didn't know coming up to me and saying that they have a disability which is unknown to me. I think that more awareness of the condition is happening but it can be frustrating when you are in your late twenties as I am. I think all people who have been diagnosed much earlier have the benefits of fewer hassles. Some people may choose to agree or disagree with me. At my age I find it difficult, as for all the years that I was undiagnosed, I knew nothing about Asperger Syndrome nor did anyone else. I find that as a seed that has existed frozen in time for all those years, it is a lot of work to catch up with my peers who are all married, have partners or who are working.

I am beginning to realize the conventions, for at my age not many young non-autistic people want to make friends, and I keep telling myself that this is the way it is. I have always found talking to myself the best solution to overcome this problem. I tell myself that I need to understand people and why I don't fit in.

When I was younger I always knew that I was different. I look back on my schooling years and don't have happy memories of either high school or primary school.

I think sometimes that those with Asperger Syndrome have been specially chosen to carry the goodness on this earth.

Garry Burge (Brisbane, Australia)
Adult with Asperger Syndrome

My life with Asperger
It is difficult to find the words to describe the effects of Asperger Syndrome, in order for people who are NT (Neurologically typical) to understand. The problem is that not being NT, I don't know what their experience is like. Of course, communication is a major problem for people with Asperger Syndrome.

Over the years, I have learned to cope with AS whilst not knowing I had it. I only found out in early 2000. I have forced myself to look people in the eye when I talk to them, as well as to take part in conversations with people whilst attempting to give the impression that I am empathetic. I can sympathize with people to a certain extent but I don't have direct access to my emotions. I sometimes use the wrong emotional response. I also cannot manage my facial expressions. If someone asks me to smile, for instance, I can't, unless I have access to a mirror. Empathy just doesn't come naturally to me. I also have to keep a watch on my tendency to steer the conversation around to my interests all the time.

I have problems deciding when to start speaking in a conversation, so I tend to interrupt the other person constantly. If several people are having a conversation and attempt to include me, I find it so focusing that I can't keep up with the conversation. By the time I have thought of something to say the topic has usually moved on. My thinking seems to slow down and people start to look at me oddly.

I recall one occasion where I was in a social situation and had been introduced to some friends of a friend of mine. They were all talking to me and my mind just sort of shut down, too much input I guess. I became incoherent and began rambling and I had to leave. This was just so embarrassing. I think that they thought I was on drugs!

With regards to my depression, I think that the reason I became depressed was lack of understanding from other people, including my parents and my brother. My brother in particular looked upon me as an embarrassment and would sometimes deny I was his brother at all.

As a teenager and when I was in my twenties I would spend hours analysing my relationships with others, trying to work out what I was doing wrong. I was constantly rejected, which severely affected my self-esteem.

It was not surprising that I became depressed. Yet when I suggested this as the cause of my depression I was told that this couldn't be the cause. How little did they know.

The anti-depressants helped a bit, along with some counselling, but the counsellor just didn't understand the way I viewed the world. I would patiently explain for instance that when I tried to relate to others it felt like a glass bell jar had been placed over me, cutting me off from other people. I just got blank looks or puzzlement.

I received various diagnoses, such as I was suffering from a number of personality disorders and neuroses. I always knew that they were wrong.

I felt like other people were a different species. As a child I even convinced myself that I was an alien, as it was the only explanation which made sense to me at the time. I was convinced that my parents had adopted me for years, as I was so unlike them.

I am glad that I finally know that I really am different from others. I always knew that I was but no one took me seriously.

I guess over the years I learnt how to deal with my problems to a certain extent. I have come a long way but still have a way to go.

Iain Payne (UK) Adult with Asperger Syndrome

(Iain has also been diagnosed as having a number of developmental disorders and anxiety)

I too, believe that understanding is really the biggest thing that we all wish for.

All my life I can remember yelling at my parents…
'You just don't understand me…'
Then came the tantrums.

Judy Darcy (Melbourne, Australia)
Adult with Asperger Syndrome

Passion Poesy

Change, Change and More Change

Change, change and more change
Of context, place and time.
Why is it that life's transient stage
Plays havoc with my mind?
You said, 'We'll go to McDonald's'
But this was just a thought.
I was set for hours,
But the plan then came to nought.
My tears and confused frustration,
At plans that do not appear,
Are painful beyond recognition
And push me deeper into fear.
How can life be so determined?
How can change be so complete?
With continuity there is no end.
Security and trust are sweet.
So, who said that change would not hurt me?
Who said my 'being' could not be safe?
Change said, 'You need continuity
In order to find your place'.
For change makes all things different,
They no longer are the same.
What was it that you really meant?
All I feel is the pain.

From the book *Life behind Glass*, a personal account of ASD
by Wendy Lawson (Southern Cross University Press,
Lismore, and NSW, Australia)

The Journey

You are driving along a highway,
a caravan of cars – all friends.
Your plan is to stick to the main highway,
your destination is mapped out.
Your car is stopped by an official.
You aren't allowed to continue, you must detour,
turn off onto a dirt track.
'But my friends are on that highway, we're following each
other' you try to explain.
You are disorientated,
and don't want to take the dirt track.
But there's no turning back, the highway is closed to you,
you have no other choice.
The track is bumpy, windy,
and a much longer drive than what was originally planned
for.
You run out of petrol, have flat tyres
and engine failure many times.
You begin to resent your friends who are on the
highway,
why didn't they have to take the detour?
Why are they cruising along?
You eventually get to your destination
and find your friends.
You are now driving side by side in different lanes.
Their trip wasn't as bad as yours, they made it earlier,
but it wasn't without its disruptions either.
You have many stories to share
about your adventurous drive,
and in the end – it has made you a seasoned traveller!

Josie Santomauro

Yellow Kite

I thought of my little child,
and realized he is just like that yellow kite
He is the kite flying free, colourful, unique, beautiful.
I like to think that the string is the love between us.

I stand and watch him, as he soars
I pull him back when danger threatens to topple him.
I give more of the string, when he needs it,
allowing him to test the skies and fly on his own.

But I love him enough to reel him in
when he is out of control
when his fears and his tears send him into a tailspin.

I pull the string gently,
I must not break the string,
for if I let it go
my beautiful yellow kite will be alone and he is not ready.

Some days there is not enough wind for my kite to fly.
On those days, when life is just too windy or even too
calm,
I fold him up carefully in my arms, hold him close,
until the time is right to let him fly free once more.

Sally Meyer (USA)

For Matt

I don't understand the things you do.
Forgive me if I can't see,
There is no rhyme or reason,
It is so frustrating for me.
You have no explanations,
for the strange things you say or do
I know it's out of your control,
I cannot put the blame on you.
Sometimes you seem so 'normal',
your behaviour right on track,
Whatever it is you try to do,
you seem to have the knack.
People think you simple minded,
but that's definitely not true,
I know you're very clever,
Sometimes it just does not show through.
So, I'm not sure how to reach you,
which disciplines to use,
No matter what the experts say,
It's the wrong one that I choose.
You are not always easy to love,
So, if I haven't said it before,
Your differences sometimes make it hard,
But I love you all the more.

So, if I make mistakes with you,
or don't appreciate your unique flair
Just remember how much that you're loved,
And how very much I care.

Sue Saladino (USA)

Madwoman Syndrome

There was a young kid with AS
Who felt under terrible stress;
But his mother (so glad)
Began to go mad
And started to write to the press.

She said that her kid, as a child
Developed autism (labelled 'mild')
AS was its name
(Asperger – the same)
And it sometimes made her kid go wild.

She had too much explainin' to do,
'Cause her kid was intelligent, too.
So few understood how this mother
– she could
Put up with this daily, anew!

All the kid wanted was just respect
From his peers (who had tried to eject
Him off of the team)
He started to scream,
But his mother knew he was correct.

Others thought he was into a fad,
Nonetheless, he was often so sad,
He would run to his room
(Like a prophet of doom!)
And this made his mother go mad.

She'd be tryin' her damnedest to cope
But she felt 'twas the end of the rope,
As she was so busy,
It made her so dizzy,
But she never gave up any hope.

'I know that my kid is real smart!'
Her words flew as fast as a dart,
'Though he's set in his ways
And is lonely, for days,
I love him down deep in my heart!'

By the grapevine, the word had
spread out,
And this mother developed a bout
Of madwomansyndrome
Right in her own home;
She knew she was mad – without doubt!

But her kid knew her well,
and said 'Here,
My dear mother, now you need not fear,
For I will survive
All the bullies, and strive
To have peace. Do I make myself clear?'

When the mother heard this,
she felt proud
Of her kid, as she said it out loud;
'I might feel like a mess,
But my kid has AS
And he stands strong right
outside the crowd!'

Brian Henson, Canada

How Do I Spell A.U.T.I.S.M?

A Anger

The first emotion I felt was anger.
Anger that this could happen to me.
I had been so careful.
I had seen my doctor as soon as I knew I was pregnant.
I took good care of myself, I didn't smoke, do drugs or drink.
I felt such rage, this was not fair!
Why had this happened to me, when other people who were not so careful had perfect children?
I was angry that this had happened to my family,
that my life would forever be different, because of this small boy.
I thought of all the years I would spend taking care of him, and how we would teach and reach him.
Other mothers had perfect children, why not me?

U Unbelief

…Denial. I lived in denial.
I wore it like a shield.
Protected myself from the pain by putting my head in the sand,
and pretending it would all go away.
I woke in the night, then it would hit me.
My child has Autism!
I stuck my fingers in my ears, trying to stop the voices in my head.
Burying my head in my pillow, refusing to believe this was happening to us.
It took forever to finally sink in, and to this day I sometimes forget, and then the realization knocks me to my knees.
It takes all my strength to get up, but I do, because I have to, for my child.

T Tears

Of course. Tears of rage, panic, frustration.
Gut wrenching tears in the middle of the night, when somehow it all seems so much worse.
In the darkness and silence of the night, it seems so much worse.
Tears are such a relief though, without them I would have gone crazy.
But I have held them back so many times.
In a store when someone makes a cruel remark, or a child approaches then turns away, with that 'look' on his face.
I refuse to cry then, because I still have my pride and although it is tattered, I cling to it like a security blanket.

I Isolation

When friends disappear and turn away. People seem to think that their child will catch 'it'. The phone stopped ringing, and people turned away at church or averted their eyes when my child had a tantrum.
The isolation is one of the most painful parts of this, being alone hurts.
My family stands beside me, and I have found friends, people who are on the same side of the fence as I am.
These people are taking the same journey, and we walk together, and that has made the difference.

S Sadness

I have felt that heart-wrenching sadness that comes with the knowledge that my child is not like other children. I have cried so many tears for him.
I have spent my waking hours worrying about him, and tossed and turned through the long night. Hours thinking about his future.
Who will care for him, when I am gone? There is so much pain involved, knowing that one day you will not be there for your child. Realizing that he will always need your care.

Sadness is a part of this path we tread, but I have found solace also.

I feel a peace inside that comes from acceptance. I cannot erase this autism, nor will I embrace it. But I have found peace, and I go on.

M Mercy and Magic

Have mercy on me, it's so hard to raise a child when others stand looking, instead of holding out a hand to help. Don't judge me when my child acts out.

Don't turn away when he screams because something has changed in his environment, and he is scared and bewildered.

I am a good mother, I may teach my child differently because he learns in a special way. It may not be the thing you would do in that situation, it may seem odd and unusual to you, but I am his mother, and I know what he needs.

I love my child just as you love yours. I have the same hopes and dreams, as you do. Please stand beside me, not behind me to judge, nor in front of me, as if to walk away.

Magic? Oh there is magic. I have seen my child blossom, I have watched his face light up, as he understands. I have rejoiced in his small steps, his smile is magic, and his heart is gold. He dances to a different tune, sometimes too sweet for me to hear, but I dance with him, and walk beside him, gratefully.

I did not choose this journey, but somehow it is mine. I must see the roses, while experiencing the thorns. I did not ask for this, but it was given to me. I must be strong enough to bear it. If I cannot persevere, then I am lost. If I give up, who will take my place?

There is joy to be found, it is not so far away.

It is in the smile, and the touch of a child.

Sally Meyer (USA)

One Hundred Tears

A hundred times I told him, a hundred times and more,
'Don't hit the dog, don't run away, don't throw that on
the floor!'

All morning he was busy, he didn't stop to think.
He broke my lamp and spilled his milk,
dumped the kitten in the sink.

He ran around the house all day without a stitch of
clothes.
He flapped his hands and laughed and cried,
and fell and bumped his nose.

At dinner came the moment when I'd simply had
enough.
He dumped his dinner on the floor and that's when I got
tough.

I sent him off to bed right then, despite his tearful pleas.
I let him cry himself to sleep – it brought me to my
knees.

When silence fell upon his room I slowly crept inside,
and gazing on his tear-stained face I broke down and I
cried.

A hundred tears I wept that night,
a hundred tears and more,
for this little boy who spilled his milk on my nice bright
shiny floor.

Why am I to scold my son for things he cannot know?
He looks to me for patience to help him learn and grow.

A hundred prayers I said that night, a hundred prayers
and more
Help me Lord to teach my child this child that I adore.

And as I left his room that night, I kissed his tears away,
and promised that tomorrow would be a better day.

(for Dhylan)

Sally Meyer (USA)

Just for this day...

Just for this morning, I am going to smile when I see your face and laugh when I feel like crying.

Just for this morning, I will let you wake up softly, in your flannel P.J.'s and hold you until you are ready to stir.

Just for this morning, I will let you choose what you want to wear, and I will say how beautiful you are.

Just for this morning, I will step over the laundry to pick you up, and take you to the park to play.

Just for this morning, I will leave the dishes in the sink, and let you teach me how to put that puzzle together.

Just for this afternoon, I will unplug the telephone and keep the computer off, and sit with you in the garden blowing bubbles.

Just for this afternoon, I will not yell once, not even a tiny grumble when you scream and whine for the ice cream truck, and I will buy you one if he comes by.

Just for this afternoon, I won't worry about what you are going to be when you grow up, or how you might have been before your diagnosis.

Just for this afternoon, I will let you help me make cookies, and I won't stand over you…trying to fix things.

Just for this afternoon, I will take you to McDonald's and buy us both a Happy Meal so you can have two toys.

Just for this evening, I will hold you in my arms and tell you the story of how you were born, and how much we love you.

Just for this evening, I will let you splash in the tub and I won't get angry when you pour water over your sister's head.

Just for this evening, I will let you stay up late, while we sit on the porch swing and count all the stars.

Just for this evening, I will bring you glasses of water and snuggle beside you for hours, and miss my favourite TV show.

Just for this evening, when I kneel down to pray, I will simply be grateful for all that I have, and not ask for anything, except just one more day.

Sally Meyer (for Dhylan)

Swim or Sink

We, as mothers, are expected to be strong, but most importantly we must look after ourselves first if we are to support our child! This is not being selfish, this is being smart. How can we look after our families if we are not capable, if we are depressed or if we are tired and confused? We hold the family together, we are the backbone of the family, if we collapse, so do they. I don't mean to sound overwhelming, but take a good look at yourself. Do you suspect you may be suffering from depression? Do you require counselling? Are you ready to deal with all aspects of Asperger Syndrome?

The main message I'm trying to get across in this section is to look after yourself. You can do this with the medium of humour, learning parenting strategies so as to gain confidence, and taking some time out for yourself.

Depression

Depression is becoming a widely acknowledged illness. Up to one in four women may suffer from depression at a stage in their lives.

Depression is when the emotion or mood of unhappiness doesn't go away, is present and affecting your everyday life.

People suffering from depression may have some of the following symptoms:

- headaches

- sleep disturbances or chronic tiredness

- lack of interest in things that normally bring you pleasure

- a change in your eating habits – more or less

- lack of self-confidence

- irritability.

If you suspect you may be suffering from mild to severe depression please see your doctor, they will be able to provide you with appropriate treatment.

As a mother , I am only too aware of the need of making time for ourselves. Too often we get so caught up with all the things that we have to do as mothers that we forget about ourselves. There's always so much to do. It's only when we feel that we can't go on any more and we begin to feel very tired that we realize we've gone too far and given far too much.

It seems to be the way of the world that mothers give and give and don't seem to need to get much back. But that supposition is wrong. It's important that we seek time out for ourselves. It's imperative that we see time out as a necessity and not slacking off from our 'motherly duties'. I suffered heavily from the 'I must not be a good mother, because I can't cope' syndrome. I felt very guilty. I wasn't coping because I wasn't allowing myself to have time out. No time out meant that I was constantly stressed. Being constantly stressed meant I didn't cope very well, and so on it went.

It's especially important that we make time out for ourselves being the carer of someone with a disability. We need to make it routine that we have some time to ourselves to regenerate and build our strength for the next onslaught. I can't stress enough how important it is to make time for us. Make it routine that you give yourself some time each day and every day. Just remember, who is going to look after our families when we are not able to? Our families need us, but they need us healthy too. So please look out for yourself and enjoy your family as they enjoy you.

Anna Tullemans, Past President, ASSN (Asperger Syndrome Support Network), Brisbane, Australia

What Now?

What happens once your child is diagnosed?

Generally a chain of events begins where there is a support system set up for your child. Schools may begin to look at the best way to support your child. You may begin to look at the best way of introducing different types of therapy to your child, such as speech therapy and social skills classes. You may also look at educating yourself in the areas of behaviour management and positive parenting.

Not only will you have the above to contend with, but you will also have the general public, family and friends who may not understand or accept your child's behaviour as a form of disability. They may prefer to judge your child as naughty or spoiled, or proceed to tell you that they 'need a good smack!'

Dealing with family, friends and the public

I used to defend my parenting skills vigilantly! I would be emotionally exhausted. I was trying to justify that my life wasn't as easy as theirs, continually justifying reasons for not attending family functions, etc. Yes, our lives do seem harder, but hey, why do we have to make a song and dance about it? If people are interested, they will ask. So I find now that I only speak about our problems/issues/good news items regarding AS and Damian if I'm asked. I have come to realize that the important thing is that we tell 'ourselves', and listen to 'us'.

Dear Josie,

Do you have any insights into how to deal with the reactions of extended family and friends? I'm getting mixed responses. Some are supportive and some think it's bunk and that Mike and I just need to parent better. I'm trying to educate and help them, but some things that are being said (and not said) are hurtful. I'm an artist and I'm drawing and painting like mad to alleviate some stress, but would love any advice if you have any.

Thanks, Kate

————————————————

Hi Kate,

I used to try to do the same thing with educating, etc., but in the end you are running around in circles, ragged, and the people who question your skills seem to be fresh as daisies! The important primary issue is that you, your husband and your child (and any siblings) understand and accept the diagnosis. Who cares about the others – at this stage, anyhow? You have to be very firm and take a stand together as husband and wife, especially when family members make comments regarding your parenting. Don't justify or defend your parenting skills, but keep repeating a phrase that you're comfortable with, e.g. 'He has a mild disability, and we are putting into place strategies to help him for his future.' (Full stop!!) You don't have to explain why, when, how, what or whatever! Be a broken record with your comment, repeat, repeat and repeat. They will eventually get the message that they can't say anything to change you, and one day they may start to show an interest, and that's the key time – when they are interested, it means that they will learn. There's no use trying to teach them now about the disability if they have 'shut-down'.

Don't let any hurtful comments in – put up an invisible shield and see them as scared and frightened people who don't want to accept any changes in 'their' lives. Just know what the truth is, and the truth is that you are doing the best for your child!

Hope this helps. Keep painting!

Josie

The Truth

'You can't tell there's something wrong, are you sure?'
(What makes you suddenly the expert?)
The truth is 'early intervention' and my child's fear of
failure is what helps him appear 'normal'.

'He has to learn to cope in today's society.'
*(You also can learn to cope with having my child
in your society.)*
The truth is you have to learn compassion.

'That's life! He has to deal with it.'
(Sure, just like you are dealing with his disability.)
The truth is that life *is* hard, show me the ideal person
who can deal with it.

'Don't worry, he'll grow out of it.'
(Not likely!)
The truth is you haven't grown out of your ignorance.

'He manipulates situations.'
(Just like you are trying to do now?)
The truth is you are keen to manipulate my child to
perform.

'You're lucky he's not as bad as some.'
(And you're lucky I forgive you.)
The truth is my child is the lucky one!

Conversation between a mother of a child
with a hidden disability and the world

Josie Santomauro

Awareness

Below is a sample card you can photocopy, cut out, fold in half and glue to carry in your wallet, or you can make up your own cards. This is a great way to create awareness of Asperger Syndrome to strangers and members of the public. Because your child may appear neurotypical members of the public sometimes believe that your child's challenging behaviour is due to behaviour management.

An example of when I used the card was when we were on public transport and Damian was tired, stressed and overwhelmed after a big day out. He wanted to get home and did not have the patience to sit on the bus. He therefore threw a public tantrum and verbally abused me. An elderly couple a few rows down whispered loudly that they thought he needed some discipline. As we approached our stop, I pulled out the card and handed it to them as we hopped off the bus.

Asperger Syndrome affects my child in their communication, behaviour and learning abilities. Therefore my child may experience difficulties in certain social situations. The result being sensory overloads which can sometimes lead to challenging behaviours. We appreciate your patience and understanding.	

Hints, ideas and strategies

- See your child's hobby/obsession as an advantage and use it when trying to put a point across, or when teaching them a strategy or as an incentive in a goal system. E.g. Damian was obsessed with Star Wars, so when we wanted him to be very interested in something we would use Star Wars characters as people or Star Wars computer games as a reward.

- Use language appropriate to your child's understanding – don't go 'over their head' with long descriptive sentences. Keep it short and sweet. E.g. if I asked Damian to do three chores, and instructed them all in a verbal row he would always hear only the first or the last chore. So now I either write it down for him, or just tell him one at a time.

- Don't all talk at once to the child. This can sound like a muffled room full of people at a party and can be very confusing for the child. It is a good idea for one person to speak at a time, turn taking so the child can listen and absorb the information.

- Use visual charts, timetables, rosters, etc. Damian had a morning and afternoon roster, so he could organize himself to and from school. This helped him become independent and in later years he did not require the visuals any longer as he could think for himself, he had learned it all by rote. When preparing a visual chart, timetable or roster, photographs of the child 'doing' are best, otherwise computer graphics are acceptable.

- When introducing a new activity or routine, draw a 'What do I do' visual story. E.g. in primary school Damian was to catch the school bus on his own. We drew up a visual story with step by step of what he was to do, and this also included some 'what ifs', e.g. what if the bus didn't come, etc. We made a large story about 'Catching the Bus', and also had one reduced down in size for him to keep in his school bag/pocket so he could refer to it. It was a huge success, and he became independent and could catch the bus home like other, neurotypical children.

- Set realistic, achievable goals for your child. When setting goals check whether they are achievable by your child, as every child's progress is different. Also does the main goal need to be broken down into smaller goals first before it can be achieved?

- Do not join the 'angry game'. When a situation is escalating, send your child to time out and walk away, have a cup of tea and wait at least half an hour for emotions to settle down before dealing with the problem. I find that if Damian comes home with a dark mood, I leave him alone for at least half an hour. He goes straight to his room, then when he has had downtime he emerges to talk to me. If I am in his face when I know that he is in a dark mood, then he will just become aggravated and take his day's frustrations out on me.

- If you feel that all is failing, please don't hesitate to ask for help, don't wait for issues to escalate and possibly get out of control. There are various avenues of help: Parent-line, support groups, school counsellor, etc. Do not think that asking for help is a sign of failure. It is a sign of strength to ask for help as you are looking at solutions and not burying your head in the sand.

- Play games with your child to encourage turn taking, etc. Some great games are simple board games and card games.

- Listen to yourself – are you using positive talk? Sometimes we need to hear ourselves and others around us – are we speaking positively or negatively? If we expect these children to learn to be positive, then we need to model this behaviour.

- Eventually, parents will need to share the diagnosis with their child. They will know when they are both ready. Be supportive and patient. It is very important to wait until the child is ready. There is no use in giving information when it is not required, as this can sometimes overwhelm a child who previously thought there was nothing wrong or different. There will come a day, whether the child is eight or eighteen, when they will begin to question their difference.

- If you notice your child becoming distressed, you can remind them to take themselves to time out or a quiet area to wind down. Sometimes it is best to give them a wide berth to calm down – do not attempt to deal with a situation as it is happening unless there is an issue with safety. It's always a good idea to give them time to wind down.

- Remind your child to look at their charts and timetables. If you are aware that they are struggling with a challenge and they do have a chart/timetable with that scenario, a gentle prompt is beneficial to remind them they have visual cues to help.

- Remind them of any changes or new things that are going to happen, like birthdays or lessons. Sometimes we get so caught up in what is going to happen or preparing to go somewhere that we forget to inform the child that they are included. If they have a whiteboard calendar, talk to them about it and add it to the calendar.

And a reminder the day before as well as on the day is helpful also.

- Warn your child about changes they don't know about. Changes are hard for children with AS, in particular if they were looking forward to going somewhere. It can be a huge let down as they have planned the scenario over and over in their heads. So if they were looking forward to seeing the real pirate at the pirate party and then you arrive and the pirate is not coming because he is sick, take the child to a quiet area and explain calmly what has happened. Sometimes we do not know how they will react. They may accept this information or they may be triggered into a tantrum. Use behavioural management strategies if the latter happens.

- Try to tell them all about where you are going or what is about to happen. Even draw a picture for them, or write down what you know. E.g. when Damian was to attend his first school camp we went for a drive and took him to the grounds, walked around, showed him the rooms, where they would eat, etc. He also took photos and showed his class that week. We glued the photos to a chart, so he could become familiar with the campgrounds. The result was a successful camp!

- Asperger Syndrome does not mean all doom and gloom – you can have a healthy relationship with your child. Children with Asperger Syndrome have a wonderful sense of humour. Laugh and have fun with them.

The School Scene

As mentioned previously, once your child is diagnosed the education system should begin to look at the best way to support your child.

Your child spends half of their waking hours in a schooling environment, therefore they are exposed to many different types of stimuli, social aspects, rules, etc. It would be a perfect world if every child had a wonderful day at school free from social injustice, anxieties and pressures. We must work hand in hand with schools and yet keep our professional boundaries as parents representing the rights of the child.

You will always find, in your child's 12-year schooling journey that there will be the predators and the carers – in both teachers and peers. Helping your child to deal with the predators is arming them with tools for life.

You have many choices with the way your child is schooled, do not ever feel that you are locked into one type of schooling. Do your research, as well as speak with other parents. Schools who do cater for our children build up a reputation amongst support groups. Alternatively, you may choose to home school your child.

Conflicts between parents and school can arise, which sadly can become barriers to your child's best interests. To help you overcome the barriers:

- Learn more about special education and your child's rights.

- Ask for a mediator to attend all meetings if you feel it's required.

- Keep a written record of all meetings and conversations held.

- Don't fight fire with fire, be calm, like water. Water will put out a fire!

Good luck!

Your child's IEP (Individual Evaluation Plan)

Once your child is officially diagnosed, you may find that the school then introduces an IEP. Basically this is a support system for your child where the support team at school can monitor your child's progress as well as teach your child and his/her teacher strategies to cope with their day.

The usual process with an IEP is for the team, consisting of teacher, support teacher, aide, parent and others, to meet. At this meeting, goals are set that are specifically catered to your child's needs. The goals are then monitored.

Each state and country has a different system. So it is worthwhile educating yourself about the IEP (or equivalent) in your area and what your child's rights are in regards to it.

A team cannot work without co-operation from all players, therefore you, being the key player, must co-operate with the school. If they require documentation from your child's medical team, or they require further testing to be done for your child, please assist them with this process. If the school recommends you attend parenting courses, don't be offended, they may be trying to achieve an all-round positive result for your child. The school representatives may be attending many courses in educating themselves to assist your child.

P reparation

R omance – the teacher/parent partnership

O ngoing

G oals for the IEP

R oles

A nger: Why are parents angry?

M eetings

Preparation

- Before attending meetings you should prepare by collecting thoughts on the goals/ questions/etc. relating to your child's IEP.

Romance – the teacher/parent partnership

- IEP meetings are famous for their awkwardness and tension.

- Regard the meeting as a negotiation within a partnership and not a standoff or a fight.

- During the meeting, take notes, listen carefully, make eye contact, use a gentle tone in your voice, don't make assumptions, and ask for clarification.

- Be assertive, not aggressive, don't take comments personally, and the end result should be a win–win situation for all parties in the partnership.

- *Most importantly, it's about your child.*

Ongoing

- It may seem like an ongoing saga! But if you see it as a saga, you'll feel drained. See it as a positive experience and you'll feel rejuvenated by the accomplishments, even small ones, made by your child due to your positive approach to your child's IEP and goals.

Goals for the IEP

- Write down some goals that you think might benefit your child and bring them to the meeting.

- Ensure that the goals the school is considering are achievable by your child.

- Goals can range from improving social skills via group game sessions to improving your child's language/comprehension skills via modifying their schoolwork to suit their needs.

Roles

- Your paraprofessional role of parent is as important as other professionals and without each others' support the team can break down.

- The Education Department is responsible for the education of the child with ASD and is accountable to the IEP.

- The parent (who knows the child better than anybody!) is the key communicator and mediator between child and school.

- Very often the roles are reversed or totally confused. This is where people involved should be regarded as the 'team' and each player has a role. The main player is the parent but (at school) the captain is the classroom teacher, who can call for help or direct instructions from his/her support team.

Anger: *Why are parents angry?*

- When major changes to the IEP or goals are made without giving parents input.

- When the team, not knowledgeable about the situation at hand, automatically backs the teacher.

- Lack of following through/breaking promises.

- When the child is disciplined because of circumstances that have arisen due to the child's disability.

- About any problem or potential threat to the child.

- In general, 'failure to communicate'.

Meetings

- Adopt a professional approach to meetings.

- If you do not understand something, ask for clarification. Don't sit there and think that just because you didn't understand something, you're stupid and therefore don't want everyone else to think this! Stupid is sitting there and pretending you understand!

- Sometimes the meeting may overwhelm you. Write everything down, or ask permission to record the meeting on tape, so you can listen to the tape back at home.

Dear Diary...

I can't recommend highly enough the importance of writing your innermost thoughts and feelings down into a diary or journal. Writing is a way of releasing your anxieties of parenting, or a formal way of celebrating your joys of being a mother.

I started a diary from the first day of diagnosis and, looking back, it shows me that I survived, and how I survived. Most importantly I can read how my child's up and down journey was important and crucial to where and who he is today.

I encourage you to start a journal/diary and make a habit of writing in it daily/weekly. I have included a sample page (p.65) for you if you choose to record how you felt when your child was diagnosed.

I have included extracts from my personal journal during the period leading up to Damian's diagnosis that I wish to share with you.

---

8 December 1994 (my birthday)

What a wonderful birthday present I received!

The pediatrician rang me on my mobile while I was grocery shopping, and said she spoke with the preschool teacher and she was now concerned that Damian didn't have ADD but some Asberges Syndrome? Apparently very rare, but she would like him to see other specialists before they make a conclusion. I couldn't finish my shopping so paid for my items and drove home – I think I was in shock! What is this syndrome? Is it degenerative? Is he going to die?

9 December 1994

I spoke with the preschool teacher re Arsberg? Syndrome, she said it comes up once every ten years! Will get more info for me if she can. Told Damian's father...denial! 'What a lot of *&%, my son's not a freak!' then he turned on me because I had 'automatically accepted' the diagnosis. I said that I was open to it all, until something was concrete. Nobody is telling me exactly what it is yet! How dare they drop this bombshell and leave me. Who do I talk to? I feel scared and alone.

12 December 1994

Pediatrician rang and has made appointments with speech therapist, OT and child psychiatrist. I asked her about the Syndrome, she said it's a gap in the developmental area, which affects the social aspects of play, etc. Made some sense! He's such a lovely child, it hurts when he says or does something and you know that it's not 'really him'!

---

13 December 1994

Spoke with preschool teacher, she will give me some info on Aspergers, said it is a high functional autism. Today, Damian was getting confused with names, called me Daddy!

14 December 1994

Today was 'one of those days'. Damian verbally went on and on, question after question. Calling us all by the wrong names. I wonder if it had to do with that big snake lolly that Grandma gave him yesterday? He was very hyper and nervous this morning.

15 December 1994

Saw pediatrician and speech therapist today. Their conclusions, not ADD, not sure about Aspergers, they will read up on it, could be systematic prag…(I don't remember the name). I felt for Damian, he senses something when we go to these 'doctors for school'. He will be assessed by the whole team next week. Speech therapist virtually said not to worry if he hasn't a 'label' yet, but for now just to concentrate on his disadvantages.

16 December 1994

I know I'm supposed to be patient with Damian. But you lose it when you have to repeat yourself all day! Yesterday I burst into tears in front of my family, I feel so stressed about the move to Queensland, Christmas and especially Damian and his future. Especially the thought of putting electrodes to his temples to measure the brain waves (suggested by the pediatrician). Imagine doing that to him?

19 December 1994

Today Damian saw the team (OT, psych, speech therapist and pediatrician). We were at the hospital for four hours. The OT seemed to think everything was normal, except the way he understood some of her instructions. He failed the 'feely bag' activity, fear of the unknown maybe? Psych did a modern day IQ test, he was excellent with the visual testing and did as well as an eight-year-old, but verbal testing he was in trouble. Pediatrician noted that he knew the answers to some questions, but he was struggling to get the answers out. I'm glad Damian's father was there to see and hear it all. I believe now they have their doubts about Aspergers. They are going to talk it over as a group and get back to us.

22 December 1994

Yes! Aspergers!! Related to autism, high functioning. They found Damian's visual skills to be over the age of eight, verbally age of three, everything else six. Main objectives they found were language, no eye contact, social skills and obsessiveness with Batman.

Apparently we are lucky! It's not degenerative, he won't die, and Damian has been detected very early. Then the pediatrician went on to tell us that adults with this syndrome are looked on as odd or eccentric and rarely marry.

Great! Bachelor with me for life! Great Christmas present! Finding out your child has a disability!

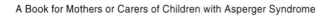

Date __ / __ / __

How I felt when my child was first diagnosed with Asperger Syndrome:

I felt sad that . . . .

I was angry that. . . . .

I felt frustrated with. . . . .

I was scared that . . . .

I was worried that. . . . .

I felt annoyed with . . . .

I didn't want . . . .

I wanted . . . .

I appreciated . . . .

I understood . . . .

I thanked . . . .

I knew . . . .

Sacred Support

Support is indeed sacred. Although the journey will be made mostly on your own, it's important to have people who you can rely on, talk with or to be there to listen to you. Trying to do this with friends or family who don't fully understand your situation is sometimes hard. This is when support groups can be called upon.

Meeting other parents with ASD children is like meeting people who have a similar cultural background to you. They understand our language, our needs, our emotional roller coaster rides, our difficulties within society and, most importantly, they understand our children.

Josie's journal

2 September 1995

Today was Damian's first session of 'Kids Club' with six other kids with AS and two teachers teaching them social skills. It was the first time we had seen other kids with AS. I sat down and couldn't help staring at them, and yet I felt comfortable looking at them. But I felt a big lump in my throat looking at Damian amongst these children – my Damian. I think his father felt the same, we're obviously still grieving. And yet, I felt more at ease today because seeing what the other kids looked like (and acted like) confirmed within my own mind that Damian was like them and we have now reached help! During the kid's session, the parents went to have coffee and I introduced Damian's father to another father who I knew to be an engineer and they hit it off – it was great.

Support groups

Individual support groups may operate differently to each other, but these are the basic aims of an Asperger Syndrome support group:

- to provide support to families and the individual with AS
- to provide information on Asperger Syndrome to parents and professionals
- to provide a resource library which includes books, videos, etc.
- to educate the community on Asperger Syndrome
- to organize workshops, seminars and guest speakers.

There are other parents out there in the same position. Find them, talk to them, they...we...*you* are the experts on our kids. Other parents know about therapies, medications, education, behaviour problems *and* solutions. The email support group has been a lifeline for me. I feel like I'm amongst long lost sisters and the similarities between our kids are *amazing*!

Marie Hoder (Nashville, TN, USA) Mother of a child with AS/ADD

You can also visit the following very informative and helpful websites:

MAAP Services for Autism and Asperger Syndrome – a non-profit organization providing information to families of individuals with autism, AS and pervasive developmental disorder.
www.asperger.org

National Autistic Society, UK – provides help, support and services to individuals with autism and their families.
www.nas.org.uk

Dr Tony Attwood – the world-renowned clinical psychologist's guide for parents, professionals and people with AS and their partners.
www.tonyattwood.com.au

Asperger Services Australia – claiming to be the world's largest support group for AS, they provide support to parents, families, carers and siblings as well as to children, adolescents and adults with AS.
www.asperger.asn.au

Josie Santomauro – author and presenter on AS, Josie also writes children's fiction under the name Josie Montano.
www.booksbyjosie.com.au

OASIS – Online Asperger Syndrome Information and Support.
www.aspergersyndrome.org

The potential success of using a parent support group to meet the specific needs of parents with ASD children will depend to some extent on the following three classes of variables: child, parents and group leader. The findings of this two-part research project suggest that (a) parents feeling that their lot in life is similar to that of other group members and (b) parent perceptions of the level of their child's difficulties were important in prompting the feeling that support group participants had a common basis for communication and sharing of information. In addition, parents reported feeling most connected and understood by group leaders who possessed a high level of autism-specific knowledge and 'hands-on' experience in dealing with ASD children.

The present research compared the relative effectiveness of generalized counselling versus strategy-based parent support groups. Parents reported the most positive effects for the latter type of parent support group and this suggests that parents benefit from learning how to apply stress management strategies as well as being provided with the opportunity to communicate about the difficulties they face.

Christopher Sharpley, PhD, and Vicki Bitsika, PhD, MAPS, Qld, Behaviour Analysis & Consulting Services, Coolangatta, QLD, Australia

Extract from conference paper titled 'Developing a support group which meets the specific needs of parents with children who have an Autism Spectrum Disorder', originally presented at the 1999 National Autism Conference, Tasmania, Australia.

The End?

Of course it's not the end.

Unfortunately we tend to only hear the difficult and heart wrenching stories about having a child with Asperger Syndrome. Laura Gilbert shares with us her son's success story; she says, 'I believe that parents and children are mutual gifts to each other.' I believe she's right! It's all about how we perceive situations brought into our lives.

I have come to understand that it's whether you perceive the gift as a problem...or the problem as a gift...

Mutual Gifts

At 15, our son is now a very articulate, witty and socially aware adolescent. After all the counselling that he has had, covering the range from psychological self-help strategies to social skill development, in many ways he is now actually more sophisticated in understanding himself and others than many of his peers.

He now has a circle of friends that he developed on his own, makes honour roll every marking period, and requires no medication nor special help in school. He has never loved school, but functions well within the school environment and often with a sense of humour.

Since art is his forte and his passion, we tell him to be patient until the day that he can devote most of his time doing what he loves.

As with all of us, our son is still a 'work in progress'. But I've come to realize that through his fears, phobias and social misperceptions, I have learned and grown and become more than I ever was before. I believe that parents and children are mutual gifts to each other. We are given, in this life, exactly what we need to become all that we are truly meant to be.

Laura Gilbert (USA) Mother
of a teenager with Asperger Syndrome

I am…

I am the little engine that did.

When on my journey in life, my tracks led me to a mountain – a diagnosis of Asperger Syndrome – I looked at it with defeat – thinking there was no way I could climb over it. Then I pondered the obstacle before me, and then I said to myself over and over, 'I think I can, I think I can…', then I slowly started climbing the mountain saying to myself over and over, 'I know I can, I know I can', and then I made it over that ominous diagnosis of Asperger Syndrome and continued my journey. I am the little engine that did.

I am more devoted than Noah's wife.

I sometimes feel overwhelmed in my 'house-boat'…365 days and 365 nights a year, constantly working with and teaching my child. But when the storms of isolation and monotony become most unbearable, I do not jump ship. Instead I wait for the rainbow that is sure to come.

I am Xena.

Real life warrior goddess of Asperger Syndrome. With my steel-plated armour I can battle anyone who gets in the way of progress for my child. I can overcome the stares and ignorance of those without a disability in their lives – and educate them as to why my child is the way he is, and why he does the things he does.

With my sword of persistence, I can battle the schools to have them properly educate my child. Yes, I am Xena – and I am prepared for any battle that might come my way.

I am beautiful.

I have hairy legs because I get no time alone in the bathroom, and bags under my eyes from staying up all night with my child. The only exercise I get is the spring from my house to my car – to take my child to therapy. Dressed up to me is, well – just that I had a moment to get dressed! They say that beauty is in the eye of the beholder – and so even on the days when I don't feel very beautiful I will know that I am…because God is my beholder.

I am Bionic Woman.

With my bionic vision I can see through the disability my child has, and see the beauty in his soul and the intelligence in his eyes – when others can't. I have bionic hearing and can look at my child when he smiles at me, and hear his voice say, 'I love you Mummy,' – even though he can't talk. Yes, I am thankful to be bionic.

I am Mary.

A not so well known mother of a child with Asperger Syndrome who was brought here to touch the souls of those around him, in a way that will forever change them. And it started with me. By teaching me things I would never have known, by bringing me friendships I never would have had, and by opening my eyes as to what really matters in life. Things like the Joy of just living in the moment, the Peace of knowing that God is in control, never losing Hope, and knowing an unconditional Love that words cannot express. Yes, I too am blessed by a special child, just like Mary.

I am Superwoman.

I am able to leap over tall loads of laundry in a single bound, and run faster than a speeding bullet, to rescue my child from danger. Oh yes, without a doubt, I am Superwoman.

I am Moses.

I was chosen to be a mother of a child with Asperger Syndrome. I may at times question whether I am the right 'man' for the job...but God will give me the faith I need to lead my child to be the best he can be. And like Moses, God will give me the small miracles here and there, needed to accomplish my mission.

I am Stretch Armstrong.

A mum that can be stretched beyond belief – and still somehow return to normal. I can stretch limited funds to cover every treatment and therapy that insurance won't. I can stretch my patience as I bounce from doctor to doctor in a quest to treat my child. I can stretch what time I have, and share it with my husband, my children, and my church and still have some leftover to help my friends. Yes, my name is Stretch. And I have the stretch marks to prove it!

I am Rosa Parks.

I refuse to move or waver in what I believe is right for my child...simply because my view is the minority, not the majority. I refuse to believe 'What can one mother do?' But instead, I will write, call, and rally to the government if I have to, and do whatever it takes to prevent discrimination against my child and ensure that he gets the services he needs.

I am Hercules.

The Greek god known for strength and courage. The heavy loads I must carry would make others crumble to the ground. The weight of Sorrow, Fear at uncertainty of the future, Injustice at having no answers, and from Tears of despair, would alone possibly be too much, even for Hercules. But then the Joy, Laughter, Smiles, and Tears of pride – at my child's accomplishments – balance the load to make it easy to bear.

I am touched by an Angel.

An Angel who lives in a world of his own. And it's true. He lives in a world of innocence and purity. A world without hatred or deceit. A world where everyone is beautiful and where no one is ugly. A world where there is always enough time. A world where he goes to bed with no worries of tomorrow and wakes up with no regrets of the past. Yes, I most certainly am touched by an Angel, and in some ways his world is better…

I am a true 'Survivor' – the mum of a child, who has faced, is facing, and will face…some of the most difficult challenges life has to offer. I am ready for the challenge and have God given endurance to last until the end, along with a sense of humour to cope with all the twists, turns and surprises along the way. Oh yes, I am a *true* 'Survivor' – and I don't need to win a million dollars to prove it!

I am a mum of a child with Asperger Syndrome, all the above, and so much more. Some days I will want to be none of the above – and just be a typical mum with a typical child, doing typical things. On those days I will know it's OK to be angry, and to cry, and to lean on my family, friends, and church for support.

Because after all, the most important thing I am, is human.

And on this day, and any other day I need to, I will read this as a reminder, of just who it is, I am…

'I am...' a piece of creative writing by Michelle Guppy of TX, USA. Michelle was the force behind the widely successful 2000 Autism Awareness Rally held in Washington DC. 'I am...' touches all mothers of children with Asperger Syndrome. (For this publication the word 'Autism' has been replaced with 'Asperger Syndrome'.)

Moving from diagnosis to discovery

Unlike diagnosis, the term discovery often refers to the identification of a person's strengths or talents. Actors are discovered. Artists and musicians are discovered. A great friend is discovered. These people are identified by an informal combination of evaluation and awe that ultimately concludes that this person – more than most others – possesses admirable qualities, abilities and/or talents. It's an acknowledgement that, 'you know, he's better than me at…'. In referring to people with respect to their talents or abilities, politically correct 'people first' terminology is not required; labels like musician, artist or poet are welcomed and considered complimentary.

If Asperger Syndrome was identified by observation of strengths and talents, it would no longer be in the DSM IV, nor would it be referred to as a syndrome. After all, a reference to someone with special strengths or talents does not use terms with negative connotations (it's artist and poet, not artistically arrogant or poetically preoccupied), nor does it attach someone's proper name to the word syndrome (it's vocalist or soloist, not Sinatra's Syndrome). Focusing on strengths requires shedding the former diagnostic term, Asperger Syndrome, for a new term. The authors feel that Aspie, used in self-reference by Liane Holliday Willey in her book, *Pretending to be Normal* (1999), is a term that seems right at home among its talent-based counterparts: soloist, genius, aspie, dancer.

The discovery of aspies brings into focus valuable, endangered opportunities that have repeatedly marched past without adequate notice of their potential. There is the opportunity to make new friends, a chance to consider those who may seem comparatively awkward, but decidedly more honest and genuine. In addition to discovering new friendships there is the opportunity to utilize unique perspectives and talents to tackle problems. There's work to do in the following century – diseases to cure, environments to save, freedoms to preserve. Fortunately, there are people with minds capable of the challenge, with the ability to focus and persevere. They possess perspectives and talents unique enough to solve the biggest of problems, or enhance the most challenging projects. They are aspies. They are living proof that the best places to play will always be those that are discovered.

Carol Gray (USA) and Tony Attwood (Australia), extracted from 'The Discovery of "Aspie": Criteria by Attwood and Gray' *Morning News* (a publication of Jenison Public Schools, Michigan) *11*, 3 (Fall 1999).